The Target is Behind the Sky

Fifty Poems of Kabir

Sunil Uniyal

BOOKS FOR ALL

Delhi

First Published 2012

ISBN 13: 978-81-7386-294-6
ISBN 10: 81-7386-294-X

Published By

BOOKS FOR ALL

(an imprint of Low Price Publications)
A-6, Second Floor, Nimri Commercial Centre,
Ashok Vihar Phase-4, Delhi - 110 052 (India)
Tel.: +91 11 2730 2453 Fax: +91 11 4706 1936
website: www.Lppindia.com
e-mail: info@Lppindia.com

Printed At
D K Fine Art Press P Ltd.
Delhi-110052

PRINTED IN INDIA

Dedicated to

To All Seekers of Truth

wherever they are

Introduction

Sant Kabirdas or Kabir (circa 1398-1518) was a leading light of the great devotional movement that swept across India during the fifteenth and sixteenth centuries. He spent most of his life in and around Benares in North India. According to some legends, he was abandoned by his Hindu mother soon after his birth and was brought up by a Muslim weaver. He came into contact with Ramananda, a Hindu sage, fairly early in his life and was soon drawn towards the teachings of the *Upanishads* and the Sufis. In due course of time, Kabir established his own order, the *Kabirpanth*, which harmonised Hinduism and Islam by preaching a universal path. Kabir believed in one attributeless God and held that one's liberation from the endless cycle of births and death is possible when the individual soul (*jivaatmaa*) merges with the Universal Soul (*Parmaatmaa*). An apostle of peace and a votary of non-violence, Kabir condemned animal slaughter, dogmas and rituals as well as worship of idols. He was strongly opposed to religious fanaticism of both the Hindus and Muslims and attacked the rigours of the caste system and social evils like widow-burning (*sati*). Kabir was thus far ahead of his time. His poems (*padas*) and couplets (*dohas*) in vernacular Hindi (Avadhi dialect) were compiled by his followers in the '*Bijak*'. Many of his songs have found their way into the holy book of the Sikhs, the *Guru Granth Saheb*, and are popular among the Indian masses even today.

In doing these translations, I have derived great help from the works of Kabir Parakh Sansthan, especially the notes and explanations given by Shri Abhilash Das in his '*Kahat Kabir*'. My indebtedness to him cannot be really expressed in words. My thanks are also due to my wife Deepa and to my sister Prof Ranu Uniyal of Lucknow University for offering their valuable suggestions from time to time. I am also grateful to Shri Alok Rawat, IAS, for his unstinted support and encouragement and to Shri Pradeep Mittal of Low Price Publications for bringing out this book in a very short time.

Sunil Uniyal, New Delhi

Contents

1.

Guru Govind dovoo khade kaake laagon paanya,

Balihaari Guru aapno jin Govind diyo bataaya

If the Guru and the Lord appear before me

to whom shall I first offer salutation?

Sure, it'll be to my Guru,

who has graced me with Lord's revelation.

2.

Guru bin kaun bataave baat

Bhraanti pahaadi nadiyaa bich men ahankaar kee laat

Kaam-krodh do parvat thaade, lobh chor sanghaat

Mad matsar kaa meghaa barsat, maayaa pavan badh thaat

Kahat Kabir suno bhai saadho, kyon tarnaa yah ghaat.

But for the Guru who is there

to show you the way?

The path you've chosen is one where

greed and anger stand like mountains,

between which the river of confusion flows,

dammed up by your tall ego

Where lust like a thief lurks around,
clouds of pride and envy rain
and the breeze of illusion blows

Says Kabir, listen, O wise one,
isn't it absurd
to walk this path to cross the world ?

3.

Lagan bin jaage naa nirmohi

Binaa lagan kee preet baavri os neer jyon dhoyi

Ham to rahte Raam bharose, razaa kare so hoyi

Bin kirpaa satguru na paave, laakh jatan kare koyi

Kahat Kabir suno bhai saadho, Guru bin mukti na hoyi.

The Unattached One will not awaken

if you have no devotion, O fool

Love without feeling is indeed

like washing oneself with dew-drops

We are all dependant on God,
what He has willed that only happens

How much hard you may try
without His grace the Guru isn't found

Says Kabir, listen O wise one,
salvation without a Guru isn't around

4.

Rahnaa nahin desa biraana hai

Yah samsaar kaagad kee pudiyaa, bund pare ghul jaanaa hai

Yah samsaar kaante kee baadi, ulajhi-ulajhi mari jaanaa hai

Yah samsaar jhaad aur jhaankhad, aag lage bari jaanaa hai

Kahahin Kabir suno bhai saadho, sadguru gyaan thikaanaa hai.

Nothing abides in this alien land

This world is like a papery wrap

that dissolves in the drops of water

It is like a hedge full of thorns
wherein one dies if entangled

It is indeed all bush and thickets
that quickly burn when caught in fire

Says Kabir, listen O wise one,
only in the teachings of the true Guru
is to be found an abiding abode

5.

Jaani boojhi saanchhin taje, karain jhoot soo nehu

Taaki sangati Raamji supinai hee jini dehu

He who befriends falsehood, forsaking truth deliberately

O Lord, even in my dream, grant me not his company

6.

Tu to Raam sumir jag ladne de

Koraa kaagaz kaalee syaahi, likhat padhat vahi padhne de

Haathee chalat apnee gati men, kuttaa bhunkai to bhunkne de

Chandi Bhairav Sitalaa devi, Dev pujai to pujne de

Kahain Kabir suno bhai saadho, narak parai vahi parne de.

Let the world go on arguing,

Friend, you just seek the Lord

On a paper blank with ink all black

those who want to read and write, let them do so,

Friend, you just seek the Lord

As an elephant goes on his way
not minding the barking dogs,
Friend, you just seek the Lord

Those who worship gods and goddesses,
let them do so, Friend, you just seek the Lord

Says Kabir, listen, O wise one,
if someone is keen to plunge into hell, let him do so,
Friend, you just seek your Lord

7.

Gagan kee ot nisaanaa hai

Dahine soor chandramaa baayen, tinke beech chhipaanaa hai

Tan kee kamaan surat kaa rodaa, shabd-baan le taanaa hai

Maarat baan bidhaa tan hee tan, Sadguru kaa parvaanaa hai

Maaryo baan ghaav nahi tan men, jin laagaa tin jaanaa hai

Kahain Kabır suno bhai saadho, jin jaanaa tin maanaa hai.

The target is behind the sky

The sun's on the right, the moon on the left-

in between it remains hidden

This body is a bow the mind its string
and the Word, its arrow- aimed straight

The messenger of the True Guru - that it is -
this arrow has pierced all bodily impurity

ı his arrow doesn't any injury inflict -
they know who have indeed felt it

Says Kabir, listen O wise one,
those who have known
they only acknowledge it

8.

Chaturaaye Hari naa milen, ai baataan kee baat

Ek nisprahi nirdhaar kaa, gaahak Gopinaath.

The truth of all truths is this:

God is not reached through cunningness;

He loves those who have no desire,

who are utterly meek and helpless

9.

Bande kar le aap niberaa

Aapu jiyat lakhu aap thaur karu, muve kahaan ghar teraa

Yah avsar nahin chetahu praanee, ant koi nahin teraa

Kahahin Kabir suno ho santo, kathin kaal ko gheraa.

O Slave, liberate yourself

Where are you and where's your home-

find it in your lifetime, Man

If you fail to wake up now

you'll be helpless when the end comes

Says Kabir, listen O wise one,

the seige of Death is hard to withstand

10.

Avadhoo andhaadhund andhiyaaraa

Yaa ghat antar baag bageechaa, yaahi men sirjanhaaraa

Yaa ghat antar saat samundar, yaahi men nau lakh taaraa

Yaa ghat antar heeraa motee, yaahi men parkhanhaaraa

Yaa ghat antar anhad garje, yaahi men uthat phuhaaraa

Kahat Kabir suno bhai saadho, yaahi men guru hamaaraa.

Friend, there is darkness all around

For people don't realise:

within this body are the gardens and groves

within it the Gardener resides

Within it also are the seven seas and countless stars

as well as the pearls and diamonds and the Jewel-maker

The drums of the Eternal within this body beat

within it is also the fountain of love

Says Kabir, listen O wise one,

within me is also my Master's dwelling

11.

Mainvaasaa moyee kiyaa durijan kaadhe doori
Raaj piyaare Raam kaa, nagar basyaa bhari poori

Let your ego be killed
and from your heart all lust be banished
Only when you are filled with devotion
God's kingdom in you will be established

12.

Saadho yah murdon kaa gaaon

Tan dhari koi rahan na paavai, kaako leeje naaon

Peer mare paigambar marihain, marihain zindaa jogee

Raajaa marihai parjaa marihain, marihain baid aur rogee

Chandaa marihain sooraj marihai, marihain dharni akaashaa

Chaudah bhuvan ke chaudhari marihain, inahoo kee kyaa aashaa

Nau hoon marihain, dash hoon marihain, marihain sahas athaasee

Taintis kotee devtaa marihain, paree kaal kee phaansee

Ekahin joti sakal ghat vyaapak, doojaa tattva na hoyee

Kahahin Kabir suno bhai saadho, bhatak maro mat koyee

Friends, this is the village of the dead

Whoever comes here with his body doesn't remain
who has stayed, can any one name?

Saints have died, prophets too,
and even the yogis, rulers and the ruled,
healers and the healed all are gone

The moon, the sun, the earth and sky -
all will die
as also the lords of all directions

All nine planets all ten incarnations
will also meet their destruction

Countless beings and crores of gods
are also entangled in the noose of Death

Eternal is only
the One Divine Light within every one

There's no second

Says Kabir, O wise men,
don't die wandering in confusion

13.

Kaun marai kahu pandit janaa
So samujhaayi kahau ham sanaa
Maatee maatee rahai samaayee
Pavanai pavan liyaa sang laayee
Kahai Kabir suni pandit guni
Roop mevaa sab dekhai duni

Who perishes?
O learned men, just explain

Dust merges into dust
air with air flies

Says Kabir, listen O wise one,

it is this body that dies

14.

Kauno thagvaa nagariyaa lootal ho

Chandan kaath ke banal khatolnaa, taa par dulhin sootal ho

Utho ree sakhi mori maang sanvaaro, dulhaa mose roothal ho

Aaye yamraaj palang chadhi baithe, nainan aansoo chhootal ho

Chaari jane mili khaat uthaayin, chahun dis dhoon-dhoo uthal ho

Kahat Kabir suno bhai saadho, jag se naataa chhootal ho

Some thug has come to loot this city

The bride sleeps on sandalwood bed
O friend, come to comb her hair,
her groom has deserted her

The god of Death is upon her,
her eyes shed tears

Four men have lifted her cot
and soon the fire will engulf her

Says Kabir, listen O wise one,
the bride has snapped
her ties with the world

15.

Kabiraa khadaa bazaar men, liye lakutiyaa haath
Je ghar phooke aapno, chale hamaare saath

In the market Kabir stands
with a staff in his hand
Calling those who've burnt their dwellings
to join his band

16.

Ghoonghat ke pat khol re, tohe piyaa milenge

Ghat-ghat ramtaa Raam Ramaiyaa

Katuk vachan mat bol re, tohe piyaa milenge

Rangmahal men deep barat hai,

Aasan se mat dol re, tohe piyaa milenge

Kahat Kabir suno bhai saadho,

Anhad baaje dhol re, tohe piyaa milenge

Lift the veil off your face

O friend, you'll find your love

In all beings dwells the Lord

say no harsh word

O friend, you'll find your love

The palace is alight with His lamp
just be seated in your self
O friend, you'll find your love

Says Kabir, listen O wise one,
the divine drum beats within you
you'll find your Love

17.

Mori chunri men pari gayo daag piyaa

Paanch tattva kee bani chunariyaa, sorah sai band laage jiyaa

Yah chunri more maike se aayee, sasure men manuvaa khoy diyaa

Mali-mali dhoyi daag na chhootai, gyaan kaa saabun laay piyaa

Kahain Kabir daag tab chhutihain, jab saaheb apnaay liyaa

O my love, my stole is stained

Made up of five elements,

this stole has now hundreds of holes

It was gifted by my mother, but
I've sullied it at my husband's home

Repeatedly I've washed it with the soap of knowledge
but the stains have still remained

Says Kabir, the stains will go
only when the Guru washes my stole

18.

Mor heeraa hiraigayaa kachre men

Koi poorab koi pachchhim khoje, koi paani koi pathare men

Paanch pachees teen ke bheetar, laag rahe bahu phikare men

Sur nar muni yati peer-auliyaa, urajh rahe bahu nakhre men

Kahain Kabir parakh jin paayaa, baandh liyo hai anchare men

The diamond has been lost in the garbage

Some search for it in the east

some in the west

some in water some among stones

Led astray by the five senses, their habits
and impulses, men are entangled in tensions;
even the gods and sages and renunciates,
are just enmeshed in their tantrums.

But, says Kabir, he has come
to realise his diamond's true cost;
he has hidden it in his heart's mantle
and from there it won't be lost.

19.

Saadho yah tan thaath tambure kaa

Ainchat taar marorat khoontee, niksat raag hajoore kaa

Toote taar bikhari gayi khoontee, ho gayaa dhooram dhure kaa

Yaa dehi kaa garb na keejai, udi gayaa hans tambure kaa

Kahai Kabir suno bhai saadho, agam panth koi soore kaa

O wise one, this body is a lyre

When its strings are tightened and the keys screwed the Self within it breaks into a sweet tune when the strings get snapped and the keys become loose

the instrument is left to gather dust

Friend, don't take pride in this body

its swan one day will fly away

Says Kabir, listen, O brother,

rare is he who bravely walks

the arduous path that leads to Him

20.

Chiuntee jahaan na chadhi sakai, raai naa tahraay
Aavaagaman kee gam naheen, tanh saklo jag jaay

Where the ant can not climb
nor the mustard seed stay
Where's no coming nor going
there all seekers long to go

21.

Tere ghat men Raam Tu kaahe bhatke

Jaise agin basat patthar me, chamkat nahi binu patke

Jaise maakhan rahat doodh me, niksat nahi binu jhatke

Jaise madhur ras basat ookh me, niksat nahi binu katke

Kahain Kabir suno bhai saadho, Hari na mile binu atke

O friend, when the Lord is within you

why are you wandering ?

As fire is hidden in the stone
and kindles on rubbing
As butter is in the milk
and is brought forth on churning
As sweet juice from the sugarcane
oozes out on cutting

Likewise, says Kabir,
You won't meet the Lord
without your mind
towards Him turning

22.

Kasturee kundali base, mrig dhoondhe van maanhi
Aise ghat ghat Raam hain, duniyaa dekhe naahin

Forest to forest
the musk-deer is roaming
in search of the scent
that flows from his navel :
So outside our Lord we are seeking

23.

Apne ghat men diunaa baaru re

Ghat ke bheetar bahut andheraa, Brahma-agni ujiyaaru re

Jagmag jot nihaaru mandir men, tan man dhan sab bhaaru re

Jhootee jaan jagat kee aasaa, baarambaar bisaaru re

Kahain Kabir suno bhai saadho, aapan kaaj sanvaaru re

Light the lamp within your heart, O friend

It is deeply dark within,

Brighten it up with the spark of Brahma

As you gaze at the flame in the temple of your heart
All bonds of body, mind and wealth become irrelevant
Know for certain that earthly desires are false
And hence must be shunned ceaselessly

Says Kabir, O wise one,
Strive for the good of your Self

24.

Moko kahaan dhoondhe re bande,
Main to tere paas men
Naa teerath men naa moorat men,
naa ekaant nivaas men
Naa mandir men naa masjid men,
naa Kaabe Kailaash men
Naa main jap men naa main tap men,
naa main barat upaas men
Naa main kriyaa karma men rahtaa,
naheen yog sanyaas men
Khojee hoye turat mil jaavoon
ik pal hi kee talaash men
Kahahin Kabir suno bhai saadho,

sab saanson kee saans men

Why do you seek Me here and there
O fool, within you I am
Not in any idol or pilgrimage
nor in some remote dwelling anywhere

My residence is not in a temple or a mosque
Nor in the Holy Kaba or Kailash
I'm also not in rituals or fasts
Nor in yogic practice or renunciation

Who seeks Me truly
finds Me instantly

Says Kabir, listen O wise one,
God is in the breath of all beings

25.

Badaa bhayaa to kyaa bhayaa jaise ped khajoor
Panthi ko chhaayaa naheen phal laage ati door

What use
is growing tall like a palm
which gives
no shade to the weary traveller ?
Its fruit is also out of reach

26.

Ghar ghar deepak barai, takat nahin andh hai

Lakhat-lakhat lakh parai, katai jama phand hai

Kahan sunan kachhu naahi, nahin kachhu karan hai

Jeete jee mari rahai, bahuri nahin maran hai

Jogee pade viyog, kahain ghar door hai

Paasahi basat hazoor, tu chadhat khajoor hai

Brahman sichchaa detaa, ghar ghar ghaalihai

Moodh sajeevan paas, tu paahan paalihai

Aisan Saahab Kabir, salonaa aap hai

Nahin jog nahin jaap, punna nahin paap hai

Lamp glows in every house

but the blind doesn't see

Who gazes steadily at that Light
freed from bonds of death is he

Nothing is there for one to say
nothing to hear and nothing to do
One who is dead, though living,
won't face death, it is true

The yogi in his detachment says
that too far the Lord resides
And in His search you climb the palm
though with you He ever abides

The priest moves on door to door
offering sermons of faith to all
And though within you is the Life-Giver
foolishly you feed a stone idol

Says Kabir: My Lord is sweet,
Who can be easily attained indeed

Acts good or bad are not required
neither meditation nor counting of bead

27.

Ham na marab, marihai samsaaraa

hamkaa milaa jiyaavanhaaraa

Saakat marain sant jan jeevain,

bhari-bhari Raam rasaayan peevain

Hari marihain to ham hoon maribai,

Hari na marai to ham kaahe maribai

Kahain Kabir man manahin milaavaa,

amar bhaye sukhsaagar paavaa

The world will die, I won't,

for I have found my Saviour

Fools die but the wise live on

drinking as they are

the elixir of Lord's Name
If God dies I too shall die
if He doesn't, why shall I?

Says Kabir, my Guru has led
my mind to the Self,
having obtained Eternal Bliss
deathless I am

28.

Kuchha lenaa na denaa, magan rahnaa

Gahree nadiyaa naav puraanee, kevatiyaa se mile rahnaa

Paanch tattva kaa banaa peenjraa, jaame bole meri mainaa

Teraa piyaa tere tan men basaa hai, khol ke dekho nainaa

Kahat Kabir suno bhai saadho, Guru charnan lipat rahnaa

O friend, be detached and happy within

The river is deep and the boat quite old

Let the Boatman guide you

through thick and thin

Of five elements is this cage
In which is the soul-bird singing
Open your eyes and see it clear -
Your Love is within you dwelling

Says Kabir, listen, O wise one,
Cling on to Guru's feet
If you want to meet Him within

29.

Toree gathri men laage chor, batohiyaa kaa sove

Paanch pachees teen hain chorvaa, yeh sab keenhaa sor

Jaagu saveraa baat aneraa, phir nahin laage jor

Bhavasaagar ik nadee bahat hai, bin utare jaa bor

Kahat Kabir suno bhai saadho, jaagat keeje bhor

Thieves eye your baggage

O traveller, why are you sleeping?

The five senses and vices within you

are alive and making a din

Be on your guard,
your path is unknown and the time fleeting

The river of this world if not crossed
will suck you in

Says Kabir, listen O wise one,
you have to be awake
at dawn's coming

30.

Mari jaaoon maangoon nahin apne tan ke kaaj
Parmaarath ke kaarne mohi na aavai laaj

I would rather die than ask for myself favours
But ashamed I won't be if I've to beg for others

31.

Ab to amar pad paayaa hai

Dukh na dard kaal nahin vyaape,

aanand mangal gaayaa hai

Mool biju binu vriksha viraaje,

satguru alakh lakhaayaa hai

Koti bhaanu chhavi bhayaa ujaaraa,

hansa sarovar paayaa hai

Kahain Kabir suno bhai saadho,

aavaagaman mitaayaa hai

I have attained Eternal Bliss

There is no time for sorrow or pain,

for now I enjoy singing His glory

The tree of His pleasure has neither root nor seed
as revealed by the grace of the true Guru

Now there is effulgence of a million suns,
my swan has dipped in the lake of His knowledge

Says Kabir, listen O wise one,
Now comings and goings have come to an end

32.

Behdaa deenho khet ko, behdaa khetanhi khaay

Teen lok sanshai paree, main kaahi kahaun samjhaay

Fence was raised to save the crop

but now fence itself eats the crop :

How to explain it to someone

when the three worlds are in doubt ?

33.

Man laago mero yaar fakiri men

Jo sukh paayo Raam bhajan men,

so sukh nahin ameeree men

Bhali buri sab kee suni leejai,

kar gujraan gareebee men

Prem nagar men rahan hamaaree,

bhali bani aayi saboree men

haath men kundi bagal men sontaa,

chaaron dishaa jageeree men

Aakhir men tan khaak milegaa,

kahaan phirat magrooree men

Kahat Kabir suno bhai saadho,

Saahib mile saboree men

Friend, my heart now rejoices in renunciation
The bliss I've attained chanting the Lord's Name
Through riches it can never be gained

I go on with my poor living, not minding
What the people say - in praise or denunciation

My dwelling is in the city of His love
I seek solace in patient suffering
I roam around with a staff and a bowl
I have my fiefdom in every direction

O friend, in dust this life has to end
Then why with pride you are puffed?
Says Kabir, listen, O wise one,
the Lord is met in forbearance

34.

Dukh men sumiran sab karen, sukh men kare na koy
Jo sukh men sumiran kare, to dukh kaahe ko hoy

During woe everyone prays
in happiness none
If prayer is in happiness,
can woe befall one ?

35.

Nar tu paar utar kanh jaiho

Aage panth na panthi koyi, kooch mukaam na paiho

Neer naah nahin khevat kirvaa, na guna khevanhaaraa

Dharti akaas kalp kachhu naahin, naa kuchh vaar na paaraa

Yah to aapee aapaa kahiye, shunya shodh na paiho

Vilaymaan ho jaahu chhinak men, yaahu thaur binu hoiho

Baarambaar vichaar shodhi man, apne maahi samaiho

Kahain Kabir mukti nahi aage, jyon kaa tyon thahraiho

Having crossed the river
where will you go, O friend?
There's no road to tread
no traveller ahead
neither a beginning nor an end

There's no water no boat
no boatman no cord
No earth is there
no sky no time no bank no ford

You have forgotten the Self within
Your search in the void will be in vain
In a moment the life will ebb
And in this body you won't remain

Be ever conscious of this, O friend,
You've to immerse within your Self
Kabir says, salvation you won't then need
For what you are you would be indeed

36.

Hansaa sudhi karo aapan des

Jahaan se aayo sudhi bisraayo, chale gayo pardes

Vahi desvaa men jote na bovai, motee phare hames

Vahi desvaa men marai na bigde, dukh naa parat kales

Chalo hansaa baso maansarovar, motee chugo hames

Kahat Kabir suno bhai saadho, ajar amar vah des

O swan, fly back to your own country

Having forgotten from where you have come

you've ventured into an alien land.

In your country there's no ploughing nor sowing
yet the fruits of divine pleasure are ever growing

In that land there's no death or disease
nor does one meet any sorrow or misery

O swan, fly to the lake of His knowledge
to pick jewels for ever and ever

Says Kabir, listen O wise one,
that country is verily abiding and eternal

37.

Turk majeed, dehraa Hindu, aap aapko dhaay
Alakh purusha ghat bheetare, taako dvaar na paay

The Hindu goes to his temple
the Muslim to his mosque
The Invisible dwells in the heart
His door nobody knocks

38.

Paani men meen piyaasee

Mohe suni suni aavat haansee

Aatam gyaan binaa nar bhatke,

Koi Mathuraa koi Kaasee

Jaise mrigaa naabhi kasturi,

Ban-ban phirat udaasee

Jal bich kamal, kamal bich kaliyaan,

Taapar bhanvar nivaasee

So man bas tirlok bhayo hai,

Yatee satee sannyaasee

Jaako dhyaan dhare vidhi Harihar,

Muni jan sahas athaasee

So tere ghat maahi viraaje,

Param purush avinaasee
Hai haajir tehi door dikhaave,
Door kee baat niraasee
Kahain Kabir suno bhai saadho,
Guru bin bharam na jaasee

I burst into laughter
whenever I hear
that the fish is thirsty in water

Without the knowledge of Self
people just wander to Mathura or to Kashi
like the musk-deer unaware
of the scent in his navel,
goes on running forest to forest

In water is the lotus plant
and the plant bears flowers
and on the flowers are the bees buzzing
Likewise all yogis and mendicants

and all those who have renounced comforts,
are on here and hereafter
and the nether world -
contemplating

Friend, the Supreme Indestructible Being,
on whom thousands of sages meditate
And even Brahma, Vishnu and Mahesh
really resides within one's self

Though He is near, He appears afar
and that is what makes one disturbed
Says Kabir, listen O wise one,
by Guru alone is the confusion curbed

39.

Koi harijan mitaave hamaar khatka

Vrichha ek adhar men jaamaa, jad oopar palai tarkaa

Jal oopar lohaa utraane, lauki bood gayi tarkaa

Baanchat Ved bhed nahin paavat, baaton men rahtaa bhatkaa

Kahat Kabir suno bhai saadho, suyi nakh maahi jagat atkaa

Let some saint my doubts clarify

With roots above and leaves below

A tree is between earth and sky

Strange it is that iron floats

but the gourd sinks in water

People go on reading scriptures
and argue more and more
without getting to the core

Says Kabir, listen O wise one,
the world is trapped in needle's eye

40.

Das dvaare kaa pinjraa, taame panchhee paun
Rahibai ko achraj ahai, jaat achambho kaun

Ten openings are in this cage
where the soul-bird resides
It is not its exit but its
stay there that's a surprise

41.

Janam teraa baaton me beet gayo,

toone kabhoon na Krishna kahyo

Paanch baras kaa bholaa-bhaalaa, ab to bees bhayo

Makar pachisee maayaa kaaran des-vides gayo

Tees baras kee ab mati upjee, lobh badho nit nayo

Maayaa jori laakh karoree, ajahoon na tripta bhayo

Vriddha bhayo tab aalas upjyo, kab nit kanth rahyo

Sangati kabhoon na keenhi toone, virthaa janam gayo

Yah sansaar matlab kaa lobhee, jhootaa thaath rachyo

Kahat Kabir samajh man moorakh, too kyon bhool gayo

O fool, in chatter your life has gone
Lord's Name you've never recited

At five years you were a kid innocent
At twenty a full-fledged youth
Driven by desires and the illusory Maya
You wandered from place to place

At thirty as your mind matured
Your greed also grew anew
Wealth increased in lakhs and crores
But satiated you weren't at all

The older you were indolence set in
Your vocal chord too became weak
Never did you seek a saintly soul
Your life has been all in vain

The world is propelled by self-interest
False is all its man-made grandeur :
Kabir wants you to comprehend this
O fool, why you've forgotten it ?

42.

Saadho so jan utare paaraa,
jin man tain aapaa daaraa
Koyi kahe main gyaani re bhai,
koyi kahe main tyaagee
Koyi kahe main indree jeetee,
aham sabahin ko [illegible]gee
Koyi kahe main jogi re bhai,
koyi kahe main bhogee
main tain aapaa doori na daaraa,
kaise jeeve rogee
Koyi kahe dharam sab saadhe,
aur barat sab keenhaa
Aapaa ke aanti nahi nikasee,

karaj bahut sir leenhaa

Garb gumaan sab doori nivaare,

karni ko bal naahi

Kahe Kabir Saaheb kaa bandaa,

pahunchaa nij pad maahi

Friends, beyond this ocean they only go

who have cast away their ego

Some say they know

some say they are renunciates

Some claim they have conquered their senses

some, they are mendicants

Some say they are yogis, some pleasure-seekers

and some say they have performed all rituals and fasts

The knots of their ego they have not opened

the load of the world is on their head

How can one lead a healthy life

clinging on to one's own 'I' ?
Says Kabir, the Self is realised
by he who has left his ego and pride

43.

Buraa jo dekhan main chalaa, buraa na milyaa koy

Jo dil khojoon aapnaa, mujhsaa buraa na hoy

Out I went looking for a crook

but couldn't find a single guy

When I peeped into myself

none was a greater crook than 'I'

44.

Kabiraa garv na keejiye, aur na hansiye koy
Ajahoon naav samudra men, naa jaane kyaa hoy

Says Kabir, don't be arrogant
nor laugh at others in torment
Your boat itself is on a sea
who knows what is next moment

45.

Saain bin dard kaleje hoye

Din nahin chain raat nahin nindiyaa,

kaase kahoon dukh roye

Aadhee ratiyaa pichhale paharvaa,

saain bin taras rahi soye

Paancho maari pacheeson bas kari,

in men chahai koi hoye

Kahat Kabir suno bhai saadho,

satguru mil sukh hoye

Without my Beloved, my heart is sore

No respite I get in day

No sleep during the night
To whom shall I my woe lament?

I go to sleep past midnight -
My yearning for love is unfulfilled

One who has overcome his five senses
And mastered instincts five and twenty
Such a one is rare actually

Says Kabir, listen O wise one,
Real happiness is attained
When one meets a True Guru

46.

Paande, boojhi piyahu tum paanee

Jihi matiyaa ke ghar manh baithe, taa manh sishti samaanee

Haad jharee jhari good garee gari, doodh kahaan te aayaa

So le paande jevan baithe, matiyahi chhoot lagaayaa

O high born, why do you ask

one's caste while drinking water?

This house is of mud wherein you dwell,

in it has merged all creation

The milk of the cow you drink

comes through her bone and blood

So, having your lunch, O high born,

why you think

impure is this mud?

47.

Oonche kul kaa janmiyaa, karnee oonch na hoye
Subaran kalash suraa bharaa, saadhu nindit soye

What use is one's high birth
if one's conduct is not nice
the gold pitcher filled with wine
gets condemned by the wise

48.

Lokaa jaani na bhoolahu bhaai

Khaalik khalak, khalak mahi khaalik,

sab gati rahaa samaai

Avvali allah noor upaayaa,

kudrati ke sab bande

Ek noor te sab jag upajyaa,

kaun bhale kaun mande

Taa Allaa kee gati nahi jaani,

guru gud deenhaa meethaa

Kahe Kabir main pooraa paayaa,

sab ghati saahib deethaa

O Men, don't forget this:

the Creator is in His creation,
all creation within the Creator exists

His Light kindles all the lamps
All beings are at His beck and call
When the world is filled with His glow
Who is high and who is low?

No one knows the ways of the Lord
Only the Guru can explain His sweet nature
Says Kabir, I've discovered
the Lord dwelling in every creature

49.

Jyon nainan men pootlee, tyun khaalik ghat maanhi
moorikh log na jaanahin, baahari dhoondhan jaanhi

As the pupil is within the eye
the Creator does in this body reside
Fools who don't comprehend this,
go on seeking Him outside

50.

Bund jo padaa samudra men, so jaanat sab koy
Samudra samaanaa bund men, so jaane birlaa koy

This everybody knows that
water-drops make up the sea
That the sea is in a drop
only the rare one can see